Feathers on Peacock: Writings on Revolution

Dabetswe Natasha

Published by Dabetswe Natasha, 2008.
http://www.lulu.com/dabetswe

Visit author's website at http://dabetswe.wordpress.com for correspondence.

Dedicated to the people of Burma,
and the freedom fighters

Preface

This book is created out of an instinctual urge of mine to show my respect, sympathy, compassion, and most of all, gratitude, to the courageous people of Burma, who have endured many hardships to have their voices heard, and for many, just for being in existence. Freedom fighters come not just in the form of opposition soldiers, but also activists, humanitarian workers, refugees, hopeful emigrants, and the common folks who struggle each day to survive the economic hardships handed to them. We are all fighting to be free from oppression, educational and vocational incompetence, economic difficulties, insufficient health and welfare services, and our own cultural integrity.

I, too, come from Burma, though I am, by far, much more fortunate than many of my fellow people. I escaped the political and economic dishevel when I left the country in my early childhood. But the blood always run thick and fast within me. Time after time, I watch the fights for freedom come alive like wildfire. As a Burmese living overseas, there seemed so little I could do. So I wrote. I wrote poems, articles, presentations, blog posts, and short stories, and kept them close to my heart.

One day, I was revisiting some of these writings, and it became apparent that I could do some small part through my love of writing. Literature is, to me, a very special element in promoting the cause of Burma. It is one fundamental human right in action – the freedom of expression. I join with my fellow people in expressing our common voice.

While being in spirit, I recognize that tangible support is also necessary, thus all the profits from the sale of this book will go to a couple of organizations that are directly helping the people and the cause of Burma, mainly Dr. Cynthia Maung's Mae Tao Clinic at the Thai-Burma Border, and the Burmese American Democratic Alliance in San Francisco. Both groups have given substantial effort and made tremendous progress in helping the people in need, and laying the foundation for important activist work.

I thank you, the reader, for being part of this tangible support too.

Contents

Poems on Revolution

Fireflies

we are catching
fireflies

our palms cupped
arms outstretched

dancing
with winged flames

Infection

Mother, your womb is
infected

and the blood that bleeds
streams down the spine of
your body-
History's Bride's
viral invasion on her wedding day.

Your limbs eaten away by decay
until all that is left is not flesh
not bone
not even blood
just overgrown green mold.

Mother,
abandoned by
the ones you gave birth to,
wait to die while
your children wash their hands clean
after the umbilical cords are cut
for they are chains on your walls.

We watch behind the glass barricades,
hands folded,
while the disease rapes you

OvErover&oveROveRandoverand over
over and over again.

But O Mother,
the monsoon rain is the tears
breaking the silence of our

cold mourning
under the fever heat.

Our voice is too low
sobs too quiet
breaths too thin
to sheath your womb.

While they rape you over and over and over and over and over and over and

(Jewel once wrote Shush)

Shush
        Hush
I will sing a lullaby
to the muffled beats
underneath your belly.
These verses will be the bloodlines
we sire together.

We can be the cancer growth
amidst this infection.

Diaspora

All their possessions
worn on their backs-
sacks and bags and
baskets full

dusty paths and
small stones jutting out
under rubber slippers

they run miles and miles
while thatch villages incinerate
inches away from memories

bullock carts kick dirt
collar bells chime
to the shuffling of feet
against the weight of
generations under iron arms.

for the sangha (of september 2007)

last night
the moon not quite full
watched my father
as he walked in the dark

she will be full today
her fullness will weigh heavy
like a teardrop about to fall

her sorrow is too far away

while earth is a distant cousin
with his scalp littered with unsung mantras

Buddham saranam gacchami ;
Dhammam saranam gacchami ;
Sangham saranam gacchami

when she drops
there will be no splash in the sea

only a pool of black secrets

maroon harvest

the flowers are in harvest today
rubber flip-flops scattered over
tarred road smeared with
leftover crimson nectar

their fruits of labor are
golden peacocks killed for
their rainbow-colored tails
light feathers large enough for flight
to carry the voices of ghosts

their claws uprooted from
the only barrier between them
and their mother land.

the flowers are in harvest today
leather slippers planted under
hunter boots covered with
unholy indifference

their maroon skins are
blooming lotus plucked for
their compassion

soft petals to carpet the bridge
between hell and heaven
between *atta* and *anatta*
between you and i

Saffron River

Rain drops -
each one large, alone,
and heavy
race from the sky
to the earth
and join the
Saffron River.

White banks
are salt deposit -
remains of tear drops
as they leave their marks
before rushing into
the body of fluidity.

Singular members
join, unite into
the backbone of a country -
the river is the energy
feeding hungry bones.

The monsoon rain
will spill its coat onto
these skeletons
and don them in
red.
They become blood
and their fury comes alive.

Their calling pushes
a river flow
and their time will dawn.

Into the saffron river
we go.

Refugee

she is a refugee in so many ways

I.
the way she drops her eyelids
when her name is called
hides onyx windows
where history marks its graffiti

only the seal of her mauve lips will tell

II.
the jungle prints on her skin
red slashes and brown cakes on olive
complement vine-like twists of black mane

not knowing whether the water on her pores
is sweat or tear

III.
quiet moon overlooks memories
that only her sighs will describe

everything else is silence
that is where they bleed from

IV.
she draws her portrait with various mediums
and cannot settle on where to place her eyes

so she leaves the face blind

V.
the stroke of her fingers on guitar strings
resonate louder than a million essays on world politics

VI.
because she speaks the unthinkable word that set her free

Army of Dreams

Here is your army
with green tanks
and blue soldiers
and fiery grounds
burning with bullet shells
and the smoke of deserted bones.

These rifles and bayonets
held so tightly straight upward
as if the clear skies are
where the enemy sleeps
and booted toes skip,
repel against orange dirt -
what a dance!

There is nothing left here
but the humps of olive helmets
rusting underneath the banyan tree.

A Beer with MLK

If I were to answer all the questions of the universe,
I will need the oceans as my pool of ink.
No amount of gallantry can dictate my humble opinions.
Strong as they might, they might rather float away.

Ten thousand years of slavery and torture end not tonight,
silent vows of conspicuous yearnings devour my sight.
Mothers cry their tearful mourns in the bleakest light
while I, the one condemned, cannot hear a word in flight.

How numb these numbers sound against my ears,
my eyes flow jungle deep and bring to tears.
Such syllables come one by one in fear
for no other to voice but my yellow pad in gear.

O sickness! Sickness you reign!
Obnoxious skies fall pity upon me.
Dark as the cloak of heavenly spies
who spit their spite on none of their kind.

Mortals, O mortals, fail not to represent
silent moaning of treacherous lands.

*   *   *

O Sickness, your monarchy has no place,
no heirloom to pass onto our silent grounds,
no legacy to hold with heartened pride,
no promise to keep upon our supple lips.

Anarchy rules the fields of hope today.
Fantasy of morbid whispers flies away.
Reason has refused to mate with logic.
Herein ends our ode to injustice.

* * *

Martin Luther King Jr. did not have beer
in his hand when he spoke words about dreams.
I am not Black, not a Man, or a Minister (god forbids!)
and beer in me - two pints full!
Does that mean I cannot speak of equality or freedom?
Puritan souls do not own the stage.

(This poem has been previously published on WRIToracle, the online literary and arts magazine at http://www.thewrit.org.)

Essays on Revolution

In the Face of Writers

There is something stirring in me. As I held in my hands a magazine of writers spilling their words, thoughts and artistry onto printed pages, urgency and pain called out. This is my life. This is what is within me to grow. Just as many the words of my voice have been silenced by years of suppression and oppression, by decades of trained shaping of my intellect and emotions, my poetry and writings have been muffled by the gag of normalcy and the mass. What had opened these gates now? The revolution lives inside me. I need look no further than my own heart.

Can the wine taste sweeter than the liberty of unrestrained flow of thoughts scattering on paper? I am in love with the love of expression. I am in debt to the tortured soul I stowed away for all these years. The unleashing is relentless. I am hungry for the intellectual capitalization of my experiences. I simply melt myself into the grease that has been caked like crude oil on the aged copper pipes. I am invisible as I was before, but my guts are hanging out, waiting to be operated upon.

Who set these rules--what I should write and what I should not? I am the mistress of my own dungeon. If I say that my dungeon is pink, then it shall be. If I say my haven has burning fire wheels, then it is mine to visualize. It is true, we are limited by the limits of this universe. We are three dimensional beings (perhaps four dimensional if we are smart enough to incorporate time into our experiential existences). We make do with what we have within these three (or four) walls. But do not mock my creativity by reminding me of my mere humanity. I seek to transcend. What did you think my writings are for? They are more spiritual and beyond this world than I could even proclaim to understand. My psyche's elements are immortal. However, they are tied, yet again, by the limited capacities of being human. I never announce my possession of this immortality. Perhaps because I am mortal, I choose to find life within me, and the life is passion that keeps the pain alive. Living is suffering. My religion has told me so. I could not write if I have not been agonized.

The urgency and calling to remove my gag is the agony that fuels my words.

Invisible Silence

My paternal uncle lives on a one lane dirt road that wiggles from the main street of Pyay Road. At the mouth of this undulating road is the headquarters for National League for Democracy. It is a ghost office since most of the members are placed in jail. Four blocks from my uncle's house is Junction Eight, named after the neighborhood that it is located in. Junction Eight is a shopping area situated at a major intersection where one of the few traffic stoplights (with countdown numbers on the pedestrian lights) have been installed in the city even in the early years of the development of the area. An estate of luxury condominiums, a 6 story shopping and office complex, a neighborhood park, and a row of shop-houses sit at each of the four corners of the junction.

One morning in May of the year 2005, something extraordinary happened at this junction when people went about their everyday business. A chemical bomb exploded at the office complex. The glasses from the windows shattered and darted out in various directions onto the streets, embedding into the tan sun exposed skins of workers, commuters and customers. With blood draining out of their bodies, the injured ran out of the bomb scene towards safety. But where would they find safety in the land ruled by guns?

No ambulance ever arrived. There was little in Burma. The homeland security did respond. However, as they secured the area, they also quarantined everybody involved in the scene. The victims had to wait... to die from both the slow bleeding from minor wounds and deadly injuries without medical attention. Across the city, there were 2 other locations where similar bombs exploded at the same time. It was a national crisis. The government was concerned. They wanted to contain the chaos. They reported the death toll as 10. But in reality, it could have been in the hundreds. Those who lost their family members in the explosion could not even enter the site to investigate if their loved ones were indeed part of the casualties. They were prohibited from posting newspaper ads to search and locate the missing people.

The government held the anti-government revolutionary groups responsible for the crises and violence. An exiled Shan Prince Tiger Yanghwe of

Canada was blamed for the bombings. He had mailed out an electronic message to his friends on April Fool's Day, announcing the reclaiming of Burma by the Shan people and a call for celebrations. Apparently, the Burmese government had taken this joke rather seriously.

During the same time period, one military official was also attacked at his office. He was not hurt because his personal assistant covered for him and took the bullet targeted at him. The personal assistant died. The official was my mother's cousin. The attacker was another member of the military government. This is exactly what it is--a power struggle. The bombings, the killings, the gunning down of a high-ranking official in a helicopter a couple of years ago, the assassination, imprisonment and dethroning of previous military intelligence leader, his family and business associates within the past year, are all about power struggles within the corrupted dictator elite. To admit this would be to expose the cracks and vulnerability of the ruling class, and so silence was enforced. Blanketing of the truth is implemented, as it has always been in this country known for her land of pagodas, a representation of peace and tranquility.

My father returned to Burma for a much awaited trip. He had left over 20 years ago and did not have a chance to visit until now. He was present during the time of the bombings, and I thank heaven that he was not one of the casualties. He was so enthusiastic about meeting with his old friends after decades of separation, but he was treated with silence. For fear of being identified wrongly as traitorous informants by shadow informants for the government, his friends could not talk to him, a foreigner. He was not local anymore and so he was deemed dangerous in his own homeland.

As I write this piece, my tone stays as factual as I could keep it to be. Why? It is not as though the incidents and state of affairs have not affected me. When I heard the stories at the dining table, my body was aching with the pain and anger I felt within. However, my face was expressionless. This is what Burma is. The sufferings are alive inside, yet they are invisible to the surrounding world by the silence imposed upon them. This is the way to survive. It is the way the tyrant government survives, the way the powerless civilians survive, the way the hopeful overseas immigrants survive, so we can push towards the next day.

This is how I don't let my agonizing rage consume me and spill out onto these words on paper. So that I could sanely tell you, in a coherent manner, the story behind the invisible silence.

What About Revolution?

What is it about revolution? Every era, there seems to be one. It almost seems as if history is defined by the popular revolution that was occurring at each particular period. I am not interested in the why and how more than I am intrigued by the very presence of such a phenomenon. I have no answers. Rather than so, I have more questions. If there is anything I can understand from this happening, it is the non-absolute of reality.

I am no historian. A mere layperson I am. In essence, my definition of revolution is very broad. Not only the politics or arts are included, but also the general sense of ideology. My reflection is not about questioning the merit of revolution. In actuality, I support the concept of revolution. Of course, this humors me. Can I really support something I feel so ill-informed about? I am a bearer of contradictions and paradoxes. Therein lies my problem with revolution.

Staging a revolution signifies to revolt. For one to revolt, there has to be an entity or ideology to revolt against. So the Protestants revolt against the order of Catholicism. So the communist revolt against class systems and capitalism. So democrats revolt against colonialists and authoritarians. But what next? Small minority groups within democratic societies seek their own revolution against the failure of democracy to address socialist concerns. Violated groups cry for democratic reform under communist dictatorships. In the artist world, surrealism is born out of movement away from realism. Realism was an opposition of idealism. From focus on aesthetic qualities to materialistic qualities, and a return to aesthetic associations, we come in one full circle.

I am one who studies the psychic forces, and so the history of psychology I am familiar with. Similar revolving door phenomenon occurs with different schools of psychological thought. First, it was the environmental influences to human mind that were of focus, namely the spirits of the world. Then followed the biological aspects of the mind, where Hippocrates discussed the four bodily humors and how they might relate to the workings of mental illness. This school of thought denounced the environmental influences in favor of the more 'scientific evidence'. Soon enough, human race created a movement towards a more psychoanalytic understanding of the mind when Freud came along. It was seen as more humanly relevant than biological causes that dismissed the human ability to process information. Psychoanalytic theory left a lasting impression in the field, yet humans are not to be satisfied. Thus, the believers in environmental causes return with a vengeance, using scientific research as their weapon, thus creating the behavioral movement. I do not wish to tell an endless tale that is cyclical. You get the story.

As I review my observation and understanding of human's tendency to revolt, one other dictionary definition of revolution came to mind. It is one that explains revolution as an orbital motion about a point or a single complete turn. In a circle, there is no beginning and there is no end, i.e. there is no absolute. Truth is infinite. It is inseparable. One leads to another and one follows the other. All angles, every micro-degree of them, is a component of the existence of truth. A single fragment is no one definite truth, though not a fallacy in itself. Is it then not irrelevant to argue one truth against another? Would this call for revolutions to be without merit? Can I still entitle to be a believer of revolutions? I am asking for a change and turnover of the way you think about revolutions. Does it make me a hypocrite? What if my act justifies my concepts of the non-absolute?

I have no answers, only more circular questions, just my own revolution.

The Burmese Experience

memoirs: Road from Pegu

We woke up earlier than the morning fog could lift its head from the marshy grounds. In half drowsy state, my sister and I took a quick cold bath from the concrete water tank located in the backyard of my mother's friend's thatched house. Wrapped only in cotton sarongs, we dragged our sleepy feet to the bathing area. It didn't take too long for us to wet and scrub our bodies before returning to the comfort of our shelter so we could dress our chilled skins.

As I waited for the traveling party to load the white pick-up truck with the necessary supplies, I stared at the sandy dune in front of me. It was only last night that I watched two groups of men, three in each team, played one of the most fascinating tournaments in this dune. The village athletes were competing in a game of *chin lone* - a particular type of volleyball game using a ball made of woven rattan, which the players tossed using only their legs, feet and thighs. Their splendid toned calves and muscular thighs shone in the moonlight as they flipped and juggled the ball in mid-air. Half the village was at the courtyard to witness the friendly match. Such handsome men, hidden away in the daily mundane of hard labor and rural life, transformed into heroes of the night under the starry sky.

The engine of the truck roared and I joined my crew in continuation of our journey up north into the plains of Burma. The mist was still lingering when we stopped at a roadside eatery for some warm pea leaf soup (and I heard that they plucked the leaves right out of their backyard when we made our orders) accompanied by a little bit of light curry with steamed jasmine rice. It was never too early for a nice substantial meal in Burma. The taste of the pea soup was the highlight of the breakfast. Its gentle bitterness of the leaf was complemented by the sweetness of the pea in a concoction of light garlic infused broth. We ate with hands, purposefully mixing the soup and curry into the rice, adding our own humanly flavor into the mix, and delivering the savory meal piece by piece with our fingers into our mouths. The server was attentive and when we finished our meal, she provided a bowl of water for washing our hands.

As I waited for the elders to freshen up in the restroom, I watched the tranquility of the morning over the stream that ran parallel to the road. The fog hovered above the murky green water that was as still as a mirror. Once in a while, the stillness was disturbed by a herd of ducks swimming downstream and a boat rowing upstream. I absorbed the untouched beauty of the village border.

We were on the road in fair time. When we entered the dusty highway full of bumpy rocks, the fog had already left, replaced by the cheerful sun and humid air. Sitting underneath the canopy in the back of the truck, with only blankets as cushions for our sore buttocks, my sister and I brought out bags of sunflower seeds roasted in garlic, which my cousin had thoughtfully included in the travel supplies. The three of us young ladies shared the bountiful snack. The crackling sounds of teeth on kennels and slurping of seeds with our tongues joined the rattling of wheels over rocks. The mothers crooned over gossips about relatives beside us, while the men chewed tobacco and exchanged words in the front of the truck. I couldn't make out what the men were talking about. The glass window was not thin enough.

I had another flashback to a time before this trip. My friends and I were in this same pick-up truck and we were driving about town. We stopped over for a water break and I was left alone with my best friend, who later on became my first boyfriend. As we exchanged our own words of intimacy that was closer than friendship but not quite yet romance, our friends sat behind the glass window and cooed at our budding first love. They laughed at us as they watched our shared silent embarrassment from their jokes. Silence felt so intense and meant so much in those times. The noise of a traveling party felt so different in comparison to the quiet chemistry of two hearts.

The dirt of the road began to stir up a storm as the truck rolled into the drier part of the region. Soon there was a fog of orange dust filling the air, suffocating our nostrils and throats. The men rolled up their windows while the women took cover under blankets. My sister, cousin and I continued our feeding on sunflower seeds under the dark safety of the covers. This was another form of intimacy among sisters.

I was not sure how long we were sheltered under blankets but the slowing of the truck and an echoing shout from my uncle's throat prompted us to emerge from the darkness. We saw that the dust storm had subsided. We were free to breathe again. As we shook ourselves loose of dirt and grit, a bus approached the side of our truck. It was crowded with travelers on the inside. Then we saw something moved on the roof of the bus. The blue tarp that covered the bus roof from front to back rose itself and revealed the congregation of travelers sitting on the top of the bus. They too struggled to shake the orange dirt off their cover. The image was quite magnificent. It was like a lid from a can of sardines was rolled back to uncover the organisms underneath.

We cheered at the travelers on the rooftop and they greeted us back. As if jealous of our comradeship, the caravan roared out of sight soon enough, leaving our moving vehicle as the only souls on the highway.

Humor Dialogue: Hold it - It's a time bomb!

Hold it - it's a time bomb!

"But it's just a yoga bag."

"Why did you leave it behind?"

"I had forgotten about it."

"You don't just forget. Don't you read the posters in the subway stations?"

"Yes, I do."

"All unattended items are suspicious. I will have to search the bag."

"But why? Somebody reported having found my bag and so I'm here to pick it up. It's that simple."

"Are you obstructing justice?"

"No, what justice?"

"What is this? A pair of thongs - a used one at that?"

"Isn't this an invasion of privacy?"

"What are you doing with a pair of thongs? Aren't you too young for that sort of thing?"

"I'm twenty-eight. I just don't look my age. Anyway, I had to put them somewhere."

"What does it say in this letter?"

"It's a love letter."

"I can't read it."

"That's because it's in Burmese."

"What's Burmese? Is it in the Middle-East?"

"It's in some kind of middle, between India and Thailand, southeast part of Asia."

"Good enough. It's confiscated."

"For what?! That's my love letter."

"How do I know it's not a spy letter? I can't read it."

"Of course, you can't read it - it's in Burmese!"

"Why did you have to write it in Burmese?"

"Because I am Burmese."

"If you are Burmese, why are you carrying around a yoga bag with a pair of thongs, and a love letter? Isn't that a Hindu thing to do? What is your religion?"

"This is ridiculous. Just give me my bag."

"I'll have to put you under arrest for obstruction of justice. Do not resist arrest."

"You mean to say, it's a crime to be an absent-minded woman from a strange race, walk around with an item from a different culture, have some sort of sex life, write in an unknown language, and look too young for my age? Now I'm supposed to just accept that charge, hang a noose around my neck and jump to my own death? Hell, NO!"

That is how I become a fugitive.

This Is the Hypocrite That I Am

Fonts on legal forms call out
"Immigrant!
Alien!"
giant green almond eyes
naked, she waddles through
a sea of flashbulb scrutiny

sweet mother tongue
a red carpet rolled out
for her catwalk

I am not made for the mass media
that constitutes America
Burmese call it *A-may-ji-kar*,
or grandmother-spreads-open
Chinese call it *Mei-guo*,
a beautiful country

truth is
my grandmother would never stay longer
than a breath of stale air from this courtyard
this country isn't so beautiful
with its post-consumption recycled compounds
a testament to its nobility

when my mother's womb made do with them
long before they became fashionable
this is the definition of survival

nevertheless
our feet touch ground here
we are hypocrites
knighting ourselves for our struggles

we saturate our skins with
liberty and prosperity when we
feed off the flesh of international commodity
pursuing their american dreams

We suck dry the bones and spit them out
while we cannibalize our own sweet tongues

I am hypocrite
I make words my voice
and my voice a word
yet I cannot even whisper its name
ghosts of motherland haunt me
I have traded my skin

paper for plastic

I yell my name out as "Immigrant"
but I cannot bear the weight of
"Alien".

(This poem has been previously published on WRIToracle, the online literary and arts magazine at http://www.thewrit.org.)

Ethnocentric

This question asks
which fork to use for salad.

I don't know

because we used hands for meals
while growing up.

No Surname, Sir

I have
no surname, sir.
I think
that explains why
I cannot be tied down.

I come free.
This is my inheritance from history.

Dear Grandmother

her wooden comb
its teeth bit into
coconut oil soaked
silver and charcoal mane
coiled into a bun

May Gyi lived in Thalyin
her ancestors from unknown grounds
with their first steps on virgin soil
bore fruit to my mother's birth place
Kayan

purple, the color of a song
mother danced to at the embassy shows
in the land of the lion

May Gyi never liked it there
she would rather have her dusty floors
and icy water from the well
than the intergalactic crowd
and climbing stairways to the concrete cage

she would rather toil away
hiking up the unpaved dirt path
on a homage trip to the golden rock
hanging peculiarly at a mountain peak

she would rather have her grandchildren
pull out strands of silver one by one
than dye it with chemicals

rather have her wooden comb
floss her head for lice

than some western medicine
on this Burmese crown

the other day i saw a wooden comb
on my lover's vanity
and, *May Gyi*, i thought of you

do come visit me from time to time
as you had for my sister during her darkest hours
my midnight can be just as grimy too

(This poem has been previously published on WRIToracle, the online literary and arts magazine at http://www.thewrit.org.)

About the Author

Dabetswe Natasha is a Burmese–American poetic writer living in Berkeley, California. She has been writing prose and poetry for over 18 years. When not lost within herself through writing, Dabetswe Natasha dances in her room, sings in her car, dabs into a little arts and crafts, and goes about town people-watching and taking snapshots.

www.ingramcontent.com/pod-product-compliance
Ingram Content Group UK Ltd.
Pitfield, Milton Keynes, MK11 3LW, UK
UKHW041834200726
13854UKWH00003BA/1127